DK READERS

Level 2

Amazing Buildings
Animal Hospital
Astronaut: Living in Space
Boys' Life: Dinosaur Battles
Boys' Life: Tracking
Bugs! Bugs! Bugs!
Dinosaur Dinners
Earth Smart: How to Take Care of
    the Environment
Emperor Penguins
Eruption! The Story of Volcanoes
Fire Fighter!
The Great Migration
Horse Show
I Want to Be a Gymnast
Journey of a Humpback Whale
Let's Go Riding
The Little Ballerina
The Secret Life of Trees
Slinky, Scaly Snakes!
Sniffles, Sneezes, Hiccups, and Coughs
Starry Sky
The Story of Columbus
The Story of Pocahontas
Survivors: The Night the Titanic Sank
Twisters!
Water Everywhere
Winking, Blinking, Wiggling, and Waggling
Angry Birds Star Wars: Lard Vader's Villains
Indiana Jones: Traps and Snares

LEGO® DC Super Heroes: Super-Villains
LEGO® Friends: Let's Go Riding
LEGO® Hero Factory: Brain Attack
LEGO® Hero Factory: Meet the Heroes
LEGO® Kingdoms: Defend the Castle
LEGO® Legends of Chima: Tribes of Chima
LEGO® Monster Fighters: Meet the Monsters
LEGO® *Star Wars*: The Phantom Menace
Pokémon: Meet Ash's Pikachu!
Pokémon: Watch out for Team Galactic!
Star Wars The Clone Wars: Anakin in Action!
Star Wars The Clone Wars: Boba Fett, Jedi Hunter
Star Wars The Clone Wars: Chewbacca and the
    Wookiee Warriors
Star Wars The Clone Wars: Jedi in Training
Star Wars The Clone Wars: Stand Aside—Bounty
    Hunters!
Star Wars: A Queen's Diary
Star Wars: Bounty Hunters for Hire
Star Wars: Clone Troopers in Action
Star Wars: Join the Rebels
Star Wars: Journey Through Space
Star Wars: R2-D2 and Friends
Star Wars: The Adventures of Han Solo
WWE: CM Punk
WWE: Hornswoggle
WWE: John Cena
WWE: Rey Mysterio
X-Men: Meet the X-Men

Level 3

Abraham Lincoln: Lawyer, Leader, Legend
Amazing Animal Journeys
Ant Antics
Ape Adventures
Beastly Tales
Bermuda Triangle
The Big Dinosaur Dig
Boys' Life: Ghost Stories
Boys' Life: Rapid Rescue
Disasters at Sea
Extreme Sports
George Washington: Soldier, Hero, President
Greek Myths
Helen Keller
Invaders from Outer Space
Plants Bite Back!
School Days Around the World
Shark Attack!
Space Heroes: Amazing Astronauts
Spacebusters: The Race to the Moon
Spiders' Secrets
Spies
The Story of Anne Frank
The Story of Chocolate
Tiger Tales
Titanic
Welcome to China
Fantastic Four: The World's Greatest Superteam
Indiana Jones: Great Escapes
The Invincible Iron Man: Friends and Enemies

LEGO® Friends: Friends Forever
LEGO® Friends: Summer Adventures
LEGO® Hero Factory: Heroes in Action
LEGO® Hero Factory: The Brain Wars
LEGO® Legends of Chima: The Race for CHI
LEGO® Monster Fighters: Watch Out, Monsters
    About!
LEGO® *Star Wars*: Revenge of the Sith
Marvel Avengers: Avengers Assemble!
Marvel Heroes: Amazing Powers
Pokémon: Ash Battles his Rivals!
Pokémon: Legends of Sinnoh
Star Wars The Clone Wars: Ackbar's Underwater
    Army
Star Wars The Clone Wars: Forces of Darkness
Star Wars The Clone Wars: Jedi Heroes
Star Wars The Clone Wars: Yoda in Action!
Star Wars: The Battle for Naboo
Star Wars: Death Star Battles
Star Wars: Feel the Force!
Star Wars: I Want to Be a Jedi
Star Wars: The Legendary Yoda
Star Wars: Obi-Wan Kenobi, Jedi Knight
Star Wars: Star Pilot
Star Wars: The Story of Darth Vader
Wolverine: Awesome Powers
WWE: Kofi Kingston
WWE: The Big Show
WWE: Triple H
WWE: Undertaker

A Note to Parents

DK READERS is a compelling program for beginning readers, designed in conjunction with leading literacy experts, including Dr. Linda Gambrell, Distinguished Professor of Education at Clemson University. Dr. Gambrell has served as President of the National Reading Conference, the College Reading Association, and the International Reading Association.

Beautiful illustrations and superb full-color photographs combine with engaging, easy-to-read stories to offer a fresh approach to each subject in the series. Each DK READER is guaranteed to capture a child's interest while developing his or her reading skills, general knowledge, and love of reading.

The five levels of DK READERS are aimed at different reading abilities, enabling you to choose the books that are exactly right for your child:

Pre-level 1: Learning to read
Level 1: Beginning to read
Level 2: Beginning to read alone
Level 3: Reading alone
Level 4: Proficient readers

The "normal" age at which a child begins to read can be anywhere from three to eight years old. Adult participation through the lower levels is very helpful for providing encouragement, discussing storylines, and sounding out unfamiliar words.

No matter which level you select, you can be sure that you are helping your child learn to read, then read to learn!

LONDON, NEW YORK, MUNICH,
MELBOURNE, AND DELHI

Editorial Assistant Ruth Amos
Senior Editor Elizabeth Dowsett
Designers Jon Hall, Sandra Perry
Pre-Production Producer Marc Staples
Producer Louise Daly
Publishing Manager Julie Ferris
Design Manager Nathan Martin
Art Director Ron Stobbart
Publishing Director Simon Beecroft

Reading Consultant
Linda B. Gambrell, Ph.D.

Dorling Kindersley would like to thank:
Randi Sørensen at the LEGO Group and J. W. Rinzler,
Leland Chee, Troy Alders, and Carol Roeder at Lucasfilm.

First published in the United States in 2013
by DK Publishing
345 Hudson Street, New York, New York 10014

10 9 8 7 6 5 4 3
006–187443–July/13

Page design copyright © 2013 Dorling Kindersley Limited

DK books are available at special discounts when purchased in bulk
for sales promotions, premiums, fund-raising, or educational use.
For details, contact:
DK Publishing Special Markets,
345 Hudson Street, New York, New York 10014
SpecialSales@dk.com

A catalog record for this book is available
from the Library of Congress.

ISBN: 978-0-7566-8695-6 (Paperback)
ISBN: 978-0-7566-8694-9 (Hardcover)

Color reproduction by Altaimage, UK
Printed and bound in China by L.Rex

Discover more at
www.dk.com
www.starwars.com
www.LEGO.com/starwars

Contents

DK READERS

BEGINNING
2
TO READ ALONE

LEGO STAR WARS

ATTACK OF THE CLONES ™

Written by Elizabeth Dowsett

Trouble in the galaxy

Meet Count Dooku!
Once, Count Dooku protected
the galaxy, but now he is a
powerful Sith Lord.
The Sith are dangerous warriors
who are greedy and want power.

Count Dooku leads an evil
group called the Separatists.
The Separatists want to control
the galaxy.
They will fight anyone who
stands in their way.

Dark power

The Force is a form of energy.
It can be used for good,
but the Sith use the dark
side of the Force for evil.

Welcome to the Jedi

These two Jedi are Obi-Wan
Kenobi and Anakin Skywalker.
The Jedi use the Force to protect
the galaxy and keep peace.

Padawan braid

Obi-Wan Kenobi   Anakin Skywalker

Obi-Wan is a wise Jedi Master.
He is Anakin's teacher.

Anakin is Obi-Wan's Padawan.
He is learning to be a Jedi Knight.
Count Dooku used to be a
Jedi, too, but now he has turned
against the Jedi Order.

Jedi prefer to make peace
rather than fight their enemies.
If they must do battle, they use
powerful lightsabers.

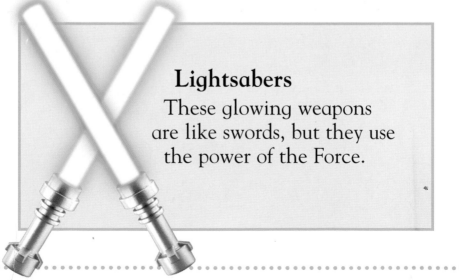

Lightsabers
These glowing weapons
are like swords, but they use
the power of the Force.

Jedi protection

Obi-Wan and Anakin have
an important Jedi mission.
They must protect Senator
Padmé Amidala on the planet
Coruscant.

Padmé may be in danger,
but she is not afraid!
She is very brave and daring.

The Senate

The Senate rules the Republic peacefully. The Senate is made up of a group of people who are called Senators.

Padmé and Anakin are childhood friends.

They are very happy to see each other after many years.

Zam Wesell's
green speeder

Assassin adventure

Help! Someone has tried
to attack Padmé.
Don't worry—Padmé is not hurt.

Obi-Wan and Anakin chase
after Padmé's attacker in a
yellow airspeeder.

Airspeeder

The Jedi are following an assassin called Zam Wesell. Before they catch Zam, someone destroys her.

Who destroyed Zam? The Jedi want to know!

Secret assassin
Assassins are paid to secretly track down and attack people.

The clone army

Look! Obi-Wan has found a huge army of soldiers.

These soldiers are identical to one another because they are human clones.
They are all copied from one man named Jango Fett.

Bounty hunter
Jango is a bounty hunter. Bounty hunters are paid to capture people.

Jango wears blue armor,
but the clones wear white armor.
Under the armor, the clone
troopers all look like Jango.

The clone army will fight for
the Republic, but it is a secret.
Sshh! Don't tell anyone.

Stop that bounty hunter!

Obi-Wan has found out that it was Jango Fett who destroyed Zam Wesell.

Watch out, Obi-Wan!

Jango fires his blaster, but clever Obi-Wan uses his lightsaber as a shield.

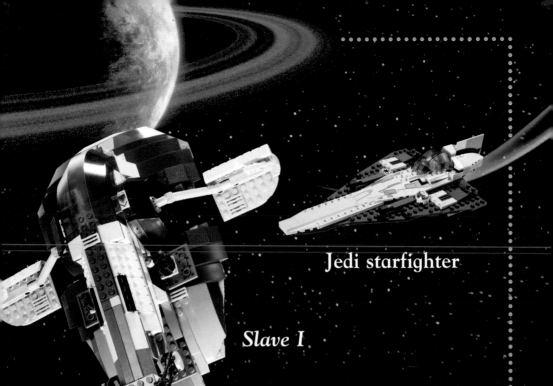

Jedi starfighter

Slave I

Jango escapes in his starship,
the *Slave I*. Whoosh!
Poor Obi-Wan doesn't like to fly,
but he chases after Jango in his
Jedi starfighter.
He follows Jango to a planet
called Geonosis.

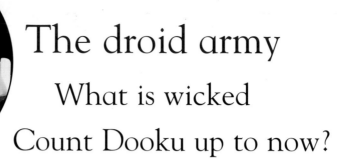

The droid army

What is wicked
Count Dooku up to now?
He is building an army of droids
to fight for the Separatists!

The droids are metal soldiers.
The smaller, yellow droids are
called battle droids.
They are not very smart.

Battle droid

Geonosians
The droid army is made
by insect-like Geonosians.
They have large wings
and big eyes, like flies.

The bigger, silver droids are
called super battle droids.
They are strong and a little
smarter than battle droids.
Beware the droid army!

Super battle droid

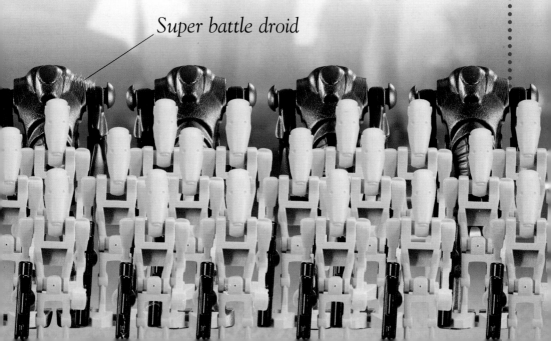

Dark secrets

Oh no! Count Dooku has found Obi-Wan on Geonosis and captured him! Energy beams keep Obi-Wan floating in a prison cell.

Count Dooku tells Obi-Wan that a clever Sith Lord has secretly taken control of the Republic.

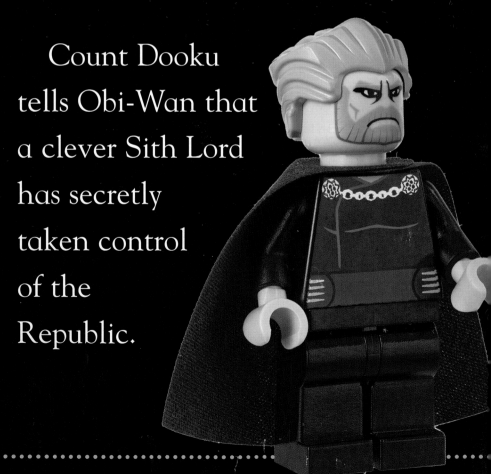

Dooku reveals
that it was this
mysterious Sith
who planned
the attack
on Padmé
Amidala.

Obi-Wan
cannot move
his arms
or legs.
He is trapped!

Jedi to the rescue!

Anakin and Padmé come to save Obi-Wan, but the Separatists capture them, too!

More Jedi arrive, led by Jedi Master Mace Windu. The Jedi rescue their friends, but then the droid army attacks!

Mace Windu

Jedi strike team

Jedi warrior

Skilled Jedi Master Mace Windu defeats
Jango Fett with his purple lightsaber.
The bounty hunter is finished, but lots of
Separatists still want to fight.

The Jedi fight bravely, but
there are too many battle droids.
Help! The Jedi are surrounded.

Droid army

Republic
gunship

The Battle of Geonosis

Look! The clone troopers have
arrived in a Republic gunship.
They will rescue the Jedi!

The clone army launches
an attack on the droids and
the Geonosians,
who fight
back!

Geonosian cannon

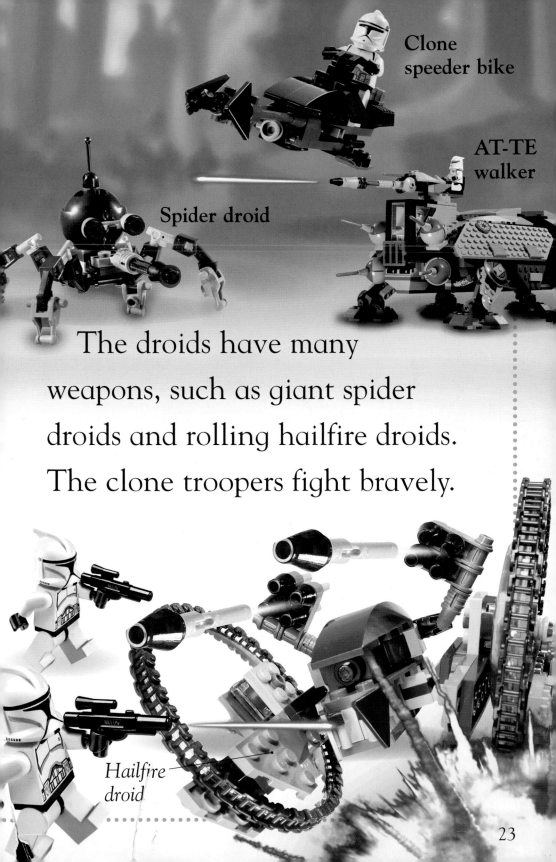

Clone
speeder bike

AT-TE
walker

Spider droid

The droids have many
weapons, such as giant spider
droids and rolling hailfire droids.
The clone troopers fight bravely.

*Hailfire
droid*

Speeder bike

Geonosian guard

Dooku's escape

Who is this running away
from the battle?
It is cowardly Count Dooku,
fleeing on his speeder bike.
Quick, the villain will escape!

Obi-Wan and Anakin follow
Count Dooku to a secret hangar.

Anakin attacks the evil
Count, but he is overpowered.
Obi-Wan then fights Dooku
in a tense lightsaber battle,
but Dooku is too powerful.
All seems lost!

Lightning duel

A small green creature comes to Anakin's rescue, just in time! This is Yoda, Grand Master of all the Jedi.

He might be very old and small, but he is very powerful.

Do not judge him by his size!

Yoda uses the Force to leap and spin around Dooku.

Count Dooku attacks Yoda
with crackling Sith lightning,
but Yoda is strong enough to
bounce it back to him!

See the lightning flash!

Dooku's master

Count Dooku is powerful, but he is not as powerful as Yoda.

The Sith Lord knows he cannot win his duel against Yoda, so he runs away! Dooku uses his Solar Sailer spacecraft to fly to Coruscant.

Solar Sailer

Now Count Dooku has a
secret meeting with a mysterious,
cloaked figure.

This is Dooku's Sith master.
He uses the dark side of the Force
to hide his identity from the Jedi.

His name is
Darth Sidious,
but who is he?
Where did he
come from?

Time to celebrate!

The Battle of Geonosis is over and Count Dooku has fled! Also, Anakin and Padmé have fallen in love.

It is against the Jedi laws to get married, but they have a secret wedding.

C-3PO

Their droids, C-3PO and R2-D2, are the only guests.

The Jedi have won the battle this time, but the Clone Wars have only just begun.
Who is Darth Sidious and when will he strike next?

R2-D2

Quiz

1. What is this fly-like creature called?

2. What type of droid is this?

3. What is the name of Jango Fett's starship?

4. Who is this green warrior?

5. Who flees in the Solar Sailer spacecraft?

1. A Geonosian, 2. Super battle droid, 3. Slave I, 4. Yoda, 5. Count Dooku

Index